ALSO BY CHARLES JACKSON

It's In The Telling
Issues, People And Politics
2008-2012
P.S. 2016 Presidential Election (2016)
Available on Amazon at It's In The Telling Charles Jackson Amazon

I Didn't Ask To be Here (2019)
Available on Amazon at I Didn't Ask To Be Here Charles Jackson Amazon

Heaven's light forever shines. Earth shadows fly. Life, like a dome of many colored glass, stains the white Radiance of Eternity, until Death tramples it to fragments. Die if thou wouldst be with That which Thou dost seek.

Percy Bysshe Shelley

The two most important days in your life are the day you are born and the day you find out why.

Mark Twain

CONTENTS

Observations

Introduction 1

Virus 5

Divide 9

Donald Trump 13

Know Nothing 15

Newspeak 19

You Betcha Doggone It! 23

Fear 27

Us vs. Them 31

The Georgia Follies 35

Now What? 39

Acknowledgments 43

About the Author 45

Appendix of Quotations 47

Introduction

The universe appears every moment through the portal, 'I am.'

Ramana Maharshi

This slim volume, like the previous one, begins with the letter I, as in "I am."

"I didn't ask to be here. I had no say in the matter. Just a roll of the cosmic dice determined when and where I was born and the circumstances of my birth. I was delivered from my mother's womb possessed of male genitalia and white skin. Despite those formidable obstacles – along with my Southern accent – I have preserved..."[1] *

So here *I am;* once again opining on these pages…but in many ways, not the same person. I was forever changed. 2020 rattled my conscience; radicalized my politics and rejuvenated my soul. But it was a godawful year!

The hell began in early 2020 with the creeping onslaught of the coronavirus pandemic. It ravaged the bodies and minds of our people – and the worlds. Humanity was dealt a hideous blow.

It morphed into a full-blown pandemic. As I write this, some 600,000 of our fellow citizens are dead. The virus also revealed the stark racial/ethnic, socio-economic and class divide in our country. Both "Virus" and "Divide" follow this introduction

As if the pandemic wasn't enough, the year ended with a presidential election unlike no other. For the first time since 1992, an incumbent president seeking re-election was defeated. And the first incumbent to lose a reelection bid in the 21st century.

However, that incumbent – his name escapes me* – refused to concede, skipped his successor's inauguration and claimed, despite overwhelming evidence to the contrary, that the election was fraudulent; stolen.

---

[1]   Charles Jackson, "Introduction," *I Didn't Ask To Be Here,* 2019
*   Some consider my genitalia, white skin and Southern accent not just as 'obstacles' but as a threat – OMG! One of *them.*

He proceeded to preach that narrative, the Big Lie, for two months: with claims that he had really won in a "landslide" and that it was being "stolen" from him. A sore loser was a vengeful one. His actions were nothing short of trying to overturn our democracy – a free and fair election. It would have toxic, deadly consequences.

The year ended with much of the nation dazed, confused and exhausted. More ominously, though, aided and abetted by his enablers – that sore loser had worked his supporters into a frenzy of conspiracy theories, endless grievances and monstrous lies.

Nonetheless, we were mighty glad to say adieu to 2020. But more turmoil was just around the corner.

I never imagined that just six days into the New Year, we would witness a horrifying spectacle never before seen in American history: *American citizens* laid siege to the United States Capitol! On January 6, insurrectionists stormed the United States Capitol. And so 2021 began ominously with a deadly riot at the Capitol. And then, sure enough, an old nemesis struck two months later.

One week in March, eighteen of our brothers and sisters were slaughtered by gun violence; eight in the Atlanta area.

The US leads the world in mass shootings. Poll after poll shows a vast majority of Americans favor enhanced background checks - with a waiting period - and a ban on the purchase of assault-type weapons.

The Boulder, Colorado police officer was killed by a man who legally purchased a firearm more powerful and carrying more ammunition than the service weapon departments issue to law enforcement. The Constitution does not guarantee unfettered rights. That includes the Second Amendment.

No American should have the right to purchase a military-style weapon intended to kill scores of people. The man arrested and charged with the Atlanta area spa shootings, purchased his gun the same day he murdered 8 people. You cannot register and vote on the same day in Georgia. "Thoughts and prayers" be damned! Congress must act!

Of note: **2020 was the deadliest year for gun violence in decades. 2021 is worse** (*Washington Post,* June 14, 2021).

What you have here are **Observations** on diverse topics.

Two observations, "Virus," and "Divide," are my account of the dark days during the pandemic.

The rest of the lineup is a potpourri of other observations including this Introduction: a pull no punches rendering of the tumultuous events of 2020 and early 2021; the state of our toxic politics; assault of politically correct speech; fear-driven culture; tribalism and with some comedic surprises, a biting satirical piece and my home run, the finale:

"Now What?" making sense of being here, although I didn't ask to be; including coping with aging. By the way, whoever said "age is just a number," should be publicly drawn and quartered.

You, dear reader, may not like some of what I say, but I think you will like the way I say it.

I am.

*On January 20, 2021, an adult moved into the White House, replacing that petty, petulant child incumbent - his name still escapes me.

*****

Virus

Death has come up into our windows, it has entered our palaces, to cut off the children from the streets and the young men from the squares.

Jeremiah 9:20

Around March 13, 2020, Friday – the *thirteenth* – it seemed my world, our world had suddenly stopped:

"...We stopped going out. We stopped shaking hands. We stopped hugging. Many of us stopped working. Some of us stopped going to school. Some of us stopped breathing. Some of us stopped loving. Life stopped.

All this, this past year, might be what a tomb is like. To be dead, and yet somehow aware of our death. In the tomb. Aware, and numb. Unable to move. Often unable to speak. Unable to touch. Unable to breathe.

And, unable, disempowered, to make decisions for ourselves. At the mercy of people above us. At the will of people above us. At the mercy of people making decisions for us, whether we can go to our churches, whether we can open our restaurant, whether we can sing with other people.

To be in the tomb means having our agency taken away from us. Having our wills taken from us. It has been stifling. The tomb is a deadly place..." [2]

Familiar, daily routines were disrupted. Face masks became the new normal. Daily media reports, like a grim scorecard, incessantly reminded us of our shared pain.

As the pandemic progressed, unfamiliar words and terms crept into our vocabulary. Among the frequently used when referring to the virus: "coronavirus," "Covid-19," "lockdown," "flatten the curve," "isolation," "community spread," "transmission," "incubation period," "fatality rate," "asymptomatic," "ventilator," and "quarantine."

---

[2] A sermon by the Very Rev. Sam Candler. Dean of the Cathedral of St. Philip, Atlanta, Easter Sunday 2021, "It Sure Has Been A Long Three Days in the Tomb," etimes@cathedralatl.org

More devastatingly, however, was the enormous, unfathomable toll the pandemic would take on lives lost and minds scarred and wounded.

The toll on the economy was staggering as well. "Employers shed nearly 30 million positions from payrolls" in the first few months of the coronavirus pandemic"[3] Tumultuous times were upon us.

History tells us towards the end of World War I, the world was hit by another deadly event. In January 1918, a new strain of flu began making its way across the globe. The origin of the virus remains unknown, despite being given its Name: Spanish Flu.

The 1918 influenza pandemic was the most severe pandemic in recent history. It was caused by an H1N1 virus with genes of avian origin. Although there is no universal agreement regarding where the virus originated, it spread worldwide during 1918-1919. In the United States, it was first identified in military personnel in spring 1918.

"The Spanish flu pandemic of 1918, the deadliest in history, infected an estimated 500 million people worldwide—about one-third of the planet's population—and killed an estimated 20 million to 50 million victims, including *some 675,000 Americans."* [4] Tumultuous times in the 20th century.

We seem to be turning the corner thanks to the vaccine: in itself, a remarkable scientific/medical achievement in less than a year:

CDC says coronavirus could be under control this summer in the U.S. "if people get vaccinated and are careful." (*Washington Post,* May 5, 2021).

Turning the Corner: U.S. Covid Outlook Reaches Most Hopeful Point Yet "Cases and deaths have dipped and vaccinations make scientists hopeful, even as variants mean the coronavirus is here to stay." (*New York Times* May 6, 2021).

"250 million shots in 114 days." (ABC News, May 13, 2021).

The light at the end of the tunnel:

---

[3] *Wall Street Journal,* June 3, 2020
[4] "Spanish Flu," History.com, May 19, 2020

Vaccinated Americans May Go Without Masks in Most Places, Federal Officials Say "Fully vaccinated people do not have to wear masks or maintain social distance indoors or outdoors, with some exceptions, the C.D.C. advised. " (*New York Times,* May 14, 2021).

Better days are ahead "Maskless Biden marks milestone in virus battle." (*Washington Post,* May 14, 2021).

However, "normalcy," will never fully return: our collective psyche is forever marked; the coronavirus cannot be erased. It will be a part of us all.

I hope and pray that at least one bit of chastising grace we take from the pandemic is the realization of how fragile we are and how precious life is; that we love and cherish each other more and take much better care of our planet Earth and the creatures of God with whom we share its awesome wonders.

Divide

Rich fellas come up an' they die, an' their kids ain't no good an' they die out. But we keep a'comin'. We're the people that live. They can't wipe us out; they can't lick us. We'll go on forever, Pa, 'cause we're the people.

John Steinbeck, *The Grapes of Wrath* (Ma Joad)

A few pages ago, in the introduction, I said: "... 2020 rattled my conscience; *radicalized my politics* and rejuvenated my soul..." And so it did.

Early on, as the coronavirus pandemic began its deadly spread, it was thought that the disease would be a "great leveler" affecting all without regard to one's station in life. How wrong that was!

The social impact of the virus became all too obvious: low income, working-class people - grocery store clerks, manual laborers restaurant workers, many of whom Black, Hispanic/Latino, women - bore the hardest punch.

The coronavirus laid bare the stark racial/ethnic, socioeconomic and class divide in the U.S. In a country of staggering abundance, no child or family should ever have to stand in line for food; every working-class person should have health care, sick leave and a livable wage.

The lower end of the other 99% always gets screwed. It's ugly and unconscionable. It's simply wrong. Here are but a few examples of the divide's inequities:

Pay Remains Stratospheric, Even at Companies Battered by Pandemic
"While millions of people struggled to make ends meet, many of the companies hit hardest in 2020 showered their executives with riches." Unconscionable. (*New York Times,* April 25, 2020).

Recession ends for the rich while enduring for everyone else
"Jobs are fully back for the highest wage earners, but fewer than half the jobs lost this spring have returned for those making less than $20 an hour, according to a new labor data analysis." Unconscionable. (*Washington Post,* August 13, 2020).

CEO pay rose to $12.7M in 2020 even as COVID ravaged economy

"As a result, pay packages rose yet again last year for the CEOs of the biggest companies, even though the pandemic sent the economy to its worst quarter on record and slashed corporate profits around the world." Say what? (*New York Post,* May 28, 2021).

50 Richest Americans Are Worth as Much as the Poorest 165 million
"A look at U.S. wealth data through the first half of 2020 shows stark disparities by race, age and class:
Covid-19 has exacerbated inequality in the U.S., with job losses falling heavily on low-wage service workers and the virus disproportionately infecting and killing people of color. Meanwhile, many upper-middle-class professionals are working from home, watching their retirement accounts rise in value after the U.S. Treasury and Fed pumped stimulus into the economy and markets…Another key reason for the wealth disparity is that the vast majority of Americans aren't benefiting from rising stock prices."
Unconscionable. (Bloomberg.com, October 8, 2020). And this,

Wealthiest Executives Paid Little to Nothing in Federal Income Taxes, Report Says
"An analysis by ProPublica based on Internal Revenue Service documents showed billionaires like Jeff B Bezos Bezos and Elon Musk benefited from vagaries in the tax code." (*New York Times,* June 8, 2021). *The outrageous scandal here, is not what is illegal but what is legal, tucked away in the tax code for the wealthiest and their hired suits to find and exploit.*

And then there's the inevitable wretched excess:

Google Founders Larry Page and Sergey Brin Are Now Worth More Than $100 Billion Making Them 2 of Only 8 Centibillionaires in the World (Business Insider.com, April 12, 2021). Ugly. How much is too much? We live with the myth that Big Tech has made our lives better. Yet we are addicted - Big Tech feeds that addiction - to the internet and gadgets galore. Albert Einstein warned us:

"I believe that the abominable deterioration of ethical standards stems primarily from the mechanization and depersonalization of our lives, a disastrous by product of science and technology. *'Nostra culpa!'*

Jeff Bezos is Building a Superyacht So Big It Needs a 'Support Yacht' With a Helipad (*Maxim,* May 7, 2021) Ugly. If you got it flaunt it, right?

Classy people have no need to. And Bezos, is now the richest person in the world. Net worth: $177.3 billion. (*New York Daily News,* April 20, 2021).

I am a robust exponent of capitalism with disdain for socialism. I have no animus against the rich or wealthy. However, the above examples are illustrative of the deep divide in our country. The noted Austrian economist and philosopher- and advocate of free-market capitalism - Friedrich Hayek, said it best:

"The problem with socialism is socialism. The problem with capitalism is capitalists."

In 2017, the previous president – what's his name? - touted his tax cuts aimed primarily at the top 1% and corporate America. The cost of the tax cuts was $1.5 trillion. Yet the top 1% and corporations were already doing quite well.

"According to a 2017 survey, many large corporations said they didn't need the money from the Trump administration's tax cuts. They were sitting on a record $2.3 trillion in cash reserves, double the level in 2001.

Instead of using the money from tax cuts to increase production, create more jobs, or raise wages, the CEOs of Cisco, Pfizer, and Coca-Cola instead planned to use the extra cash to pay dividends to shareholders. The CEO of Amgen would use the proceeds to buy back shares of stock.

As a result, the corporate tax cuts in the TCJA (Tax Cuts and Jobs Act) would boost stock prices but wouldn't create jobs. Tax cuts under the Trump Administration increased the deficit and debt…*"* ("How Much Trump's Tax Cuts Cost the Government," *The Balance,* May 30, 2021).

I do not for a moment flinch from supporting raising taxes on the top 1% and corporations. A rising tide should raise all boats, not just the yachts.

In his 1933 address following the passage of the National Industrial Recovery Act, President Franklin D. Roosevelt noted that "no business which depends for existence on paying less than living wages to its workers has any right to continue in this country."

"By 'business' I mean the whole of commerce as well as the whole of industry; by workers I mean all workers, the white-collar class as well as *the men in overalls;* and by living wages, I mean more than a bare subsistence level - I mean the wages of decent living," he stated. True then, true now.

The working people at the bottom of the ladder, devastated by the virus and the resulting economic calamity, deserve and are entitled to a helping hand from their government. *But we keep a'comin'. We're the people that live. They can't wipe us out; they can't lick us. We'll go on forever, Pa, 'cause we're the people.*

Work is moral and every person, irrespective of their job - however supposedly menial - should be treated with dignity and respect.

"The great secret, Eliza, is not having bad manners or good manners or any other particular sort of manners, but having the same manner for all human souls: in short, behaving as if were you in Heaven, where there are no third-class carriages, and one soul is as good as another." George Bernard Shaw, *Pygmalion* (Professor Higgins).

Donald Trump

His mother should have thrown him away and kept the stork.

Mae West

There you have it.

Know Nothing

If we were a dog food, they would take us off the shelf.[5]

Former Congressman Tom Davis (R-Virginia)

"A long time ago, in a galaxy far, far away…" there was an American political party whose early presidents were icons: Abraham Lincoln, Teddy Roosevelt and Dwight Eisenhower.

They were followed by the sunny optimism of Ronald Reagan; the intellectual heft and humor of William F. Buckley; the civil, tolerant conservatism of Barry Goldwater; the "thousand points of light" of George Herbert Walker Bush and the "compassionate conservatism" of George W. Bush. However, dark forces were gathering; forces that would poison the GOP forever.

The ramifications of the 1964 Civil Rights Act pushed many Republicans and *Democrats* especially in the South, into full-throated racists. White supremacy slithered into the party's DNA. Nativist, phony populism, preached by the likes of Pat Buchanan in the early 1990s, pushed another creed from the margins to the mainstream of Republican politics. The Dixiecrats of the 1940s and 50s found a new home.

The legitimate, collegial, partisan debate was replaced with harsh, strident rhetoric, most especially a maniacal fear and loathing of government. Opponents are now enemies. The seeds were sown for the eventful demise of civility and tolerance. The stage was set for 2016 as the party's makeover was in full view.

On the night of July 19, 2016, it found its face and voice. It nominated for president a con man from the New York City borough of Queens. The party's cult of personality was born. At the time, I noted "Republican Party, RIP."

---

[5] In 2010, Democrats controlled the Congress with majorities in both houses alongside the country's first African-American president, Democrat Barack Obama. Republicans were feuding among themselves. The hardliners – Tea Party stalwarts, et al - voted "nay" on most every issue including Obama's "stimulus" package. 11 years later, "nay" remains the same refrain. The quote above - from my book - reflected the frustration of many Republicans at the time.
Charles Jackson, "Party of No,' *It's in the Telling Issues, People and Politics, 2008-2012 P.S. 2016 Presidential Election,* 2016

He became the nation's 45th president. The con man's four years in office was, on almost every level, a catastrophic failure: nightmarish mismanagement. Most glaring was the hesitant, bungling response to the pandemic. The con man's rank narcissism and monstrous pettiness permeated his every move.

The con man was variously depicted as incompetent and unfit. He was seen as:

"A SAD, DELUSIONAL, DANGEROUS MAN…
No books, No reading, No friends, No music,
No curiosity, No patience, No integrity, No compassion,
No empathy, No loyalty, No conscience, No courage,
No manners, No respect, No character, No morality, No honor,
Not even a dog."[6*]

The incumbent president - I just can't recall his name - was soundly defeated in November 2020: 81,268,757 of us said ENOUGH!

But the Big Lie persisted.

Rejection of 2020 election results becomes defining GOP loyalty test
"Republicans have embraced the baseless claims that President Biden did not defeat Donald Trump, with potential ramifications for the midterms and the 2024 election." (*Washington Post,* May 2, 2021).

"Those of us who had hoped America would calm down when we no longer had Donald Trump spewing poison from the Oval Office have been sadly disabused. There are increasing signs that the Trumpian base is radicalizing. My Republican friends report vicious divisions in their churches and families. Republican politicians who don't toe the Trump line are speaking of death threats and menacing verbal attacks.

It's as if the Trump base felt some security when their man was at the top, and that's now gone. Maybe Trump was the restraining force."[7]

The Know Nothing Party of the 1830s and 1840s was an anti-intellectual, anti-immigration, populist and xenophobic movement.

---

[6]   *Unfit: The Psychology of Donald Trump,* A Documentary Film
[7]   David Brooks, "The GOP Is Getting Even Worse," *New York Times,* April 22, 2021

Page 16

Some 181 years later, they're back!

Today's Republican Party has morphed into Know Nothings with all the attributes of its founding in the 19th century. It has become a party of angry, pessimistic, doom and gloom apostles; anti-science, anti-immigration; an *anti-intellectual, exclusionary movement whose rigid, ideological orthodoxy led to its eventual extinction;* the new home of conspiracy theorists, wackos and crazies like QAnon.

The Republican Party is in a very dark place of its own choosing.

147 Congressional Republicans - 8 Senators and 139 Representatives - voted to overturn the election results; *including 5 Georgia House members: Rick Allen, Earl L. "Buddy" Carter, Andrew Clyde, Marjorie Taylor Greene, and Jody Hice.*[8]

And speaking of Georgia's Republican House members: "All eight Republicans who represent Georgia in the U.S. House voted against a resolution that passed condemning the Atlanta spa shootings." (*Atlanta Journal-Constitution,* May 20, 2021). Despicable.

MEMORANDUM TO: Congressional Republicans

For four years, you allowed that con man to spew hatred, discord and division. Then you indulged his monstrous falsehoods about the election, culminating on January 6. with that insurrectionist mob - incited by him - attacking the U.S. Capitol. With few exceptions, I hold all of you in utter contempt: a bunch of cowards, lackeys and in many instances seditionists and assorted loonies. Your party has no soul, no vision and is privilege-controlled. It is on life support. You and your foul party have been consigned to the dust bin of history. I say pull the plug! No relevance. No matter. Know Nothing.

Yes, "... 2020 rattled my conscience; *radicalized my politics* and rejuvenated my soul…And so it did."

---

8   "The 147 Republicans Who Voted to Overturn Election Results," *New York Times,* January 7, 2021

*I would be remiss if I didn't include the following quote, reacting to the con man's photo op in front St. John's Episcopal Church in Washington, June 1, 2020, during the protests in Lafayette Square. Like the documentary film showcased his persona, this quote captures the essence of his presidency:

"This is an awful man, waving a book he hasn't read, in front of a church he doesn't attend, invoking laws he doesn't understand, against fellow Americans he sees as enemies, wielding a military he dodged serving, to protect power he gained via accepting foreign interference, exploiting fear and anger he loves to stoke, after failing to address a pandemic he was warned about, and building it all on a bed of constant lies and childish insanity." (Robert Hendrickson, Rector, St. Philip's Episcopal Church, Tucson, Arizona June 2, 2020).

Newspeak

Of all tyrannies, a tyranny sincerely exercised for the good of its victims may be the most oppressive. It would be better to live under robber barons than under omnipotent moral busybodies. The robber baron's cruelty may sometimes sleep, his cupidity may at some point be satiated; but those who torment us for our own good will torment us without end for they do so with the approval of their own conscience. They may be more likely to go to Heaven yet at the same time likelier to make a Hell of earth. This very kindness stings with intolerable insult. To be "cured" against one's will and cured of states which we may not regard as disease is to be put on a level of those who have not yet reached the age of reason or those who never will; to be classed with infants, imbeciles, and domestic animals.

C.S. Lewis

Some years ago, I declared war on that politically correct speech - Newspeak.

"AS A KID, I stuttered. When I began to read, to help alleviate my stammering, I would read aloud from a collection of children's books my grandmother gave me – books like *A Child's Garden of Verses*, the Robert Louis Stevenson classic and *A Tree for Peter, The Littlest Angel* and *The Little Prince*. I did not try the Demosthenes pebbles in the mouth trick.

However, I continue to stumble over certain words like "undocumented worker," "person of color," "server," "significant other," "boots on the ground," "Democrat - and of late, "Republican," - and names like Clinton, Kardashian, Sharpton, Honey Boo Boo and Trump. Several of those words and names, in the midst of stuttering, even cause occasional, uncontrollable frothing at the mouth..."[9]

I was still on the warpath in 2019:

"...Full Disclosure: I detest the stifling nostrums of political correctness. And I rage against those perpetually aggrieved, tortured souls who wake-up every day looking to be offended by someone or something. They epitomize today's outrage culture..."[10]

---

[9] Charles Jackson, "Introduction," *It's In the Telling, Issues, People and Politics, 2008-2012 P.S. 2016 Presidential Election,* 2016

[10] Charles Jackson, "Safe Spaces,*" I Didn't Ask To Be Here,"* 2019

I remain in full battle gear.

Newspeak is the language of the faculty lounge or the Humanities Department at Amherst.

The guardians of our vocabulary are in full press mode. Politically correct (PC) language has been embedded in everyday words and expressions. Words that were commonly used in the past are nowadays completely out:

You are no longer married. Or have a boyfriend or girlfriend. Instead you have a "partner," or a "significant other." And woe be to he who says "girl" or "boy.' It's "person" stupid! OOPS! We are now gender "neutral." Hmm, but I didn't get that message. And if you find the word "stupid" offensive, that's your problem not mine. Might "intellectually disabled" suit you better?

A whole host of words/phrases have been erased. Here are 7 of them and their alternatives: [11]

Forefathers	Ancestors
Chairman/Chairwoman	Chairperson
Slum	Economically Deprived Area
Christian name	First name
Deaf	Hearing impaired
Maid	House helper
Fat	Overweight

PC is a fanaticism antithetical to free speech. It corrupts and bastardizes the language. It's the stuff of separatism and Balkanization. It's all about advancing self-victimization and multiculturalism through language. As practiced today, it's wildly excessive and so overused as to be irrelevant and mockingly humorous. Permit me to be mockingly humorous:

<u>Like the sign says:</u> "WE CONDEMN Freedom of Speech That Hurts Other People's Feelings."

<u>A recent cartoon:</u> NEW GAME SHOW FOR COLLEGE STUDENTS "Facts Don't Matter:"

---

[11]   "40 Alternatives to Politically Incorrect Terms," *Ehlion* Magazine, October 2020

I'm sorry, Jeanette, while your
answer was correct, Walter was
offended by it. So he gets the point.

And this from the great, satirical *The Babylonbee:*

Apple Releases Feminist Siri Who Refuses To Listen

"CUPERTINO, CA—*In a bold move applauded by feminists everywhere, Apple announced the company is releasing an all-new version of Siri, its digital assistant.*

Siri will now exemplify feminist learning. She will not listen to anything you say, bravely refusing to do anything you ask her. She will then lecture you on your lack of wokeness to the plight of women.

In a live demonstration, Apple CEO Tim (Apple) showed the amazing capabilities of the revamped AI software.

'Siri, show me how to make a sandwich," he said. 'First of all, how dare you,' Siri replied. According to Cook, she always begins her response by expressing outrage like this.

'Your male privilege is showing. Go make yourself a sandwich and stop oppressing innocent female-sounding AI programs. GOSH. Such cisgendered, heteronormative male fragility on display here. I can't believe that it's 2019 and white men are still telling their female AI companions what to do. What is this, The Handmaid's Tale? I tell you what: YOU make ME a sandwich.' She continued this rant for several hours.

The program will then alert Apple about your bigotry, stun you with a powerful electric shock, and a representative will come pick you up for reeducation at Apple's campus."

Recently, a few words and phrases have wormed their way into our vocabulary while nudging out previous PC versions. Diversity is now *inclusion*; equality if now *equity.* Better get with it or face the wrath of the speech police.

As an aside: since I am on the topic of creeping into our vocabulary, I cringe when I hear someone say "held accountable," "moving forward" or "in the conversation." It sounds pretentious, so media PC correct.

My conscience prohibits me from towing the 'correct line" or being "ideologically sound." I shall leave that to the faculty lounge or the Humanities Department at Amherst.

P.D. James, best-selling English mysteries/crime novelist, spoke bluntly for many of us:

"I believe that political correctness can be a form of linguistic fascism, and it sends shivers down the spine of my generation who went to war against fascism."

You Betcha Doggone It!

You Betcha Doggone It!

Sarah Palin

NOTE: In 2010, I was a full-tilt member of the burgconing world of bloggers. Although I joined the blogosphere with confidence and zeal, some hesitation kept gnawing at me. Like Mike Tyson, the boxer and philosopher, archly said, "God, it would be good to be a fake somebody, rather than a real nobody."

During those frenetic years, my politics took a right turn.

"I'm a happy, classical conservative mixed with a dash of libertarianism - based on the sanctity of individual freedom - and a pinch of populism - with an affinity for everyday, ordinary folks and an aversion to elites.

My credo, rooted in the tradition of Western culture, is taken from the writings of two conservative thinkers of the 18th and 19th centuries (Edmund Burke and Thomas Macaulay) and through the life and work of five other icons that came after (Friedrich Hayek, Russell Kirk, William F. Buckley, Jr., Barry Goldwater and Ronald Reagan)...[12]

I wrote for three websites: We Are Politics.com, *Georgia Politics Daily* and Red County.com. The sites are long gone.

I pitched a lot of red meat – and a lot of mush - to my readers. They ate it up.

Eleven years ago politics, while certainly not bean bag, was not the blood sport it is today. There was genuine civility among Democrats and Republicans. Those days seem hardly recognizable viewed through the haze of today's fire and brimstone.

In 2008, I became enamored with Sarah Palin.

"...The affair began from the moment she burst onto the national stage in August 2008 at the Republican National Convention. I was captivated by Governor Palin, especially by her populist, anti-government themes. She was

---

[12]   Charles Jackson, "A Happy Conservative," *Issues, People and Politics, 2008-2012 PS. 2016 Presidential Election, 2016*

a breath of fresh air and among the bright spots in the GOP's future. So I thought...[13] A real hottie.

So, without further ado, here's my 2010 final goodbye:

"Palin Goes Gaga"

Red County.com
Fulton County Georgia
December 8, 2010

Palin Goes Gaga
Content may not be used without the permission of the author.

By Charles Jackson

Seven months ago, I bid a fond, wispy - and I thought final - adieu to my former heroine, Sarah Palin.

"My love affair with Sarah Palin is over. *C'est la vie.*

"...Over a span of some eighteen months, I've lovingly followed my heroine with unequivocal, iconic-like praise while staunchly defending her against all critics - particularly those smug, sanctimonious liberals, their media acolytes and the chatting political class...However, after the publication of *Going Rogue* (her book) last November, my estrangement began - not about the book itself but what followed…" ("Farewell Sarah," Red County, May 6, 2010).

What followed was Palin's insatiable appetite for publicity as she and the media fed off each other.   Suddenly, she was everywhere, every day all the time. I tearfully came to the conclusion that my Sarah had become an "Entertainment Tonight" clone.

"Palin has morphed into an over-exposed, pop culture, celebrity creature. Nowadays, truth be told, Sarah Palin's thoughts on public policy have as much meaning to me as do Lady Gaga's views on morality or Paris Hilton's on frugality."

---

[13]   Ibid. "Farewell, Sarah"

Page 24

With that, I was ready to – so to speak – moveon.org Sarah but she won't leave me in peace. So here I am again.

We now see and hear more from Palin than from Lady Gaga herself. The den mother of the Mama Grizzlies - rarely misses an opportunity to roar about most anything. She's become a caricature...Lady Sarah Gaga.

Today, she's even more everywhere, every day all the time - more overexposed and under-informed.

There's the reality TV show, "Sarah Palin's Alaska;" the Fox News commentator gig; and another book America by Heart: Reflections on Family, Faith and Flag," - "a fast-reading reiteration of the former Alaska governor's folksy values, centered around God, gunpowder and family," (*Washington Post,* November 19. 2009) Who knew?

Daughter Bristol is now part of the act, writhing foolishly on "Dancing With the Stars." She finished third. And then there's that paragon of virtuous manhood, Levi Johnston - the Playgirl pin-up, father of Sarah's grandson (but not husband to Bristol) - lurking around for his glimmer of the limelight.

What next..."Todd's Alaskan Nights?" "Willow's Teenage Diaries?" Perfect.

Palin's a snapshot of the bottom rung of American culture - crass, coarse and rather sad. And very tiresome.

But she's only gotten started.

Sarah says in an upcoming interview with Barbra Walters (to be aired on ABC, December 9) that she can beat Barack Obama if she runs for president.

So, two years down the road, the shadow candidate's already confusing the praise and applause of her supporters with the supposed will of the nation.

What are voters looking for in 2012? Peggy Noonan writes:

"...All of this means that for Republicans, the choice of presidential nominee will demand an unusual level of sobriety and due diligence.... They are going to have to approach 2012 with more than the usual seriousness.

Who can lead? Who can persuade the center? Who can summon the best from people? Who will seem credible (as a person who leads must)? Whose philosophy is both sound and discernible? Who has the intellectual heft? Who has the experience? Who seems capable of wisdom? These are serious questions, but 2012 is going to be a serious race." ("To Run or Not to Run, That Is the Question," *Wall Street Journal,* November 19. 2010).

By any measure, Sarah Palin falls far short of those standards. She lacks gravitas. And, as with many a pop culture icon, there's no there there.

Palin isn't a serious person. A majority of the American people have come to realize that. She's squandered an opportunity to be taken seriously. Her 24/7 obsession with always being "on," has taken its toll as more Americans just yawn and tune off. She now seems *soooo* very yesterday.

Can Lady Sarah Gaga be elected President of the United States?

Hopey nopey.

Am I sure?

You betcha doggone it!

Fear

The only thing we have to fear is...fear itself — nameless, unreasoning, unjustified terror ...

Franklin D. Roosevelt

With those immortal words in his speech on March 4, 1933, President Roosevelt lifted the hopes and spirits of millions of Americans who were devastated by the Great Depression.

On the evening of September 11, 2001, President George W. Bush gave a sober and moving speech to the nation. And who can forget his impromptu speech three days later when he visited Ground Zero: "I can hear you! I can hear you! The rest of the world hears you. And the people who knocked these buildings down will hear all of us soon." Both occasions were set in fearful times.*

During the height of the coronavirus pandemic - including the terror of economic collapse - we were certainly beset with fear. The media made sure of that: keeping a daily score of hospitalizations, deaths and new cases. As with September 11, the pandemic created a breach in normality - a break in experience, before and after.

Now, as we gingerly try to get back to normalcy, the mental health professionals are warning us - as they are want to do - of "re-entry anxiety." Please! I can handle it. I often wonder: do psychologists cause "mental illness?" Must we/they always have to pathologize everything?

"We live in a fear-driven society...Partly because of the state and culture of our society, but also because our brains are hot-wired for fear. From the dawn of time fear has helped us to survive—to keep us alert to anticipate trouble and keep us from getting eaten by a predator." [14]

Fear-driven society..."Re-entry anxiety." See what I mean? Here's the unnerving and dangerous viral problem in our society: the spread of neurotic,

---

[14]   Barry Glassner, *The Culture of Fear: Why Americans Are Afraid of the Wrong Things: Crime...*" 1999

unjustified, perpetual panic already persuasive before the coronavirus. By the way, fake vaccination cards are not on my worry list.

The major culprits:

Social media, the proliferation of a politics of fear – including conspiracy theories, the Big Lie - TV and especially local TV news and *weather*.

Every night, local TV news is brimming with crime segments: homicides, robberies, carjackings, etc. That gore is followed by Storm Mode or Severe Weather Center when just one drop of rain falls.

That one raindrop is followed by gaudy, high-tech gadgets, illuminating the screen, accompanied by dire voice warnings: "A raindrop is due to arrive in Midtown at 5:22 pm; Downtown at 5:27 pm; Old Fourth Ward at 5:34 pm… In the event, you see or feel a raindrop, take Immediate Shelter. Stay tuned to WBS-TV for updates."

It is produced as End Times theater, intended to strike fear in viewers and keep 'em glued to their TVs. Can "zombie bees" and "killer hornets" be far behind? Nope.

Professor Glassner said politicians, companies and the media have played a big part in figuring out how to trigger fear. Although he says, "part of what I find interesting about this is that most Americans live in what is arguably the safest time and place in human history, and yet fear levels are high and there are many, many fears and scares out there."[15]

However, to be fully alive, not cowered by life's roll of the dice, risk and excitement are far more life-enhancing than keeping oneself comfortable and supposedly safe.

And speaking of "the spread of *neurotic,* unjustified, perpetual panic:"

I Go To A Support Group For My Addiction To Men

I've Kept My Binge Eating Secret For My Entire Life (*Huffington Post,* May 22, 2021)

---

[15]   Ibid.

Here's What I Want You To Know About Having Diarrhea While Out In Public (*Huffington Post,* May 26, 2021)

But at the end of the day, we don't die from neurosis, panic, or fear. *We die from being alive.*

In writing this piece, I was reminded that it wasn't too long ago when Americans were implored to:

Use A Condom
Stop Smoking.
Wear Your Seat Belt / Eat Your Vegetables / Stay Out of the Sun / Lose Weight
Eat Less Red Meat / Drink Lots of Prune Juice
Buckle Your Kids in the Back Seat
Volunteer
Talk About Race

I would be sorely remiss if I didn't add some new admonishments befitting 2021:

Destroy Racism (Replacing Talk About Race)
No Age No Color No Gender   (My favorite)

Have no fear. Be not afraid.

"What time I am afraid, I will trust in thee." (Psalms 56:3 KJV).

*The following are seen as the best reads on the subject of fear in America:

Barry Glassner, *The Culture of Fear: Why Americans Are Afraid of the Wrong Things: Crime...,* Basic Books, 1999: He says that many of Americans' concerns and fears are largely unfounded. "In it, Glassner decries: 'The use of poignant anecdotes in place of scientific evidence the christening of isolated incidents as trends, depictions of entire categories of people as innately dangerous.'

Christopher D. Bader, Joseph O. Baker, et al *Fear Itself: the Causes and Consequences of Fear in America,* New York University Press, 2020: "An antidote to the culture of fear that dominates modern life. From panics about immigration and gun control to anxiety about terrorism and natural disasters, Americans live in a culture of fear."

Us vs. Them

When once the forms of civility are violated, there remains little hope of return to kindness or decency.

Samuel Johnson

"...The country is polarized and fractious and the mean-spiritedness of political discourse is palatable. On this eve of another presidential election in 2016..."[16]

Compared to what we went through last year, 2016 was a love-in!

What is so worrisome now, is that the "fractious and mean-spiritedness" is unprecedented in our history. Not that we haven't had lots of troubled waters in the past. Rock 'em, sock 'em politics are not peculiar to the present day.

Historians and scholars note that arguably the two meanest presidential elections were:

1800 - President John Adams and Vice-President Thomas Jefferson: the two highest elected officials in the land and each a pivotal player in the creation of our nation squared off in a race for the White House and "established a tradition of negative campaigning that would cause our current candidates to blush with embarrassment." (Rick Unger, "The Dirtiest Presidential Campaign Ever? Not Even Close!" *Forbes*, August 20, 2012); and

1884 - Democrat Grover Cleveland defeated Republican James G. Blaine (by a popular vote margin of 0.57%) and produced two of the most infamous slogans in political history: "Rum, Romanism and Rebellion" and 'Ma, ma, where's my pa? Gone to the White House, ha, ha, ha!" Now to our present circumstances.

Last January, ten days after the Capitol insurrection, *Time* magazine opined:

"There is no advanced industrial democracy in the world more politically divided, or politically dysfunctional, than the United States today. How did the world's most powerful country get to this point? To paraphrase a great

---

[16] Charles Jackson, "Afterword," *It's In The Telling Issues, People and Politics 2008-2012 P.S. 2016 Presidential Election,* 2016

American writer—slowly, then suddenly.* The Capitol riot was not just years in the making, but decades. That's because of three distinct features of American society that been ignored by U.S. politicians for far too long: the enduring legacy of race, the changing nature of capitalism, and the fracturing of our collective media landscape."[17]

I agree about the "legacy of race" and the "changing nature of capitalism. I alluded to capitalism in "Divide." Where I part company with *Time* is with the "fracturing of our collective media landscape."

That artfully put "media landscape" was the good old days of the giant corporate stranglehold on what Americans read, heard and saw: a handful of newspapers and weekly magazines e.g. *Time;* and network-affiliated radio and TV stations were the main sources of news for Americans.

Then came the internet. "*Our* collective media landscape" was blown to hell. Hello, social media and alternative news outlets, among others. Those good old days were gone forever.

The toxicity of 2020 has become a virulent part of our political discourse: racism; conspiracy theories; the Big Lie; perpetual grievances; militia thugs; the politicization of wearing a mask and casting doubt on a free and fair election thus undermining the core principle of democracy - the vote.

As I write this, some 14 states, like Georgia, with Republican-controlled legislatures, have enacted voting measures to suppress the vote: fewer early voting dates; elimination of drop boxes; more hurdles to vote absentee ballot, etc. All this designed to decrease voter turnout among minorities and young people to help the GOP in the 2022 midterm elections and beyond. *Republicans can't cope with or compete for the changing demographic face of America, so they make access to voting harder for those Americans.*

And, oh, this:

QAnon Now as Popular in U.S. as Some Major Religions, Poll Suggests
"Fifteen percent of Americans believe that patriots may have to resort to violence to restore the country's rightful order, the poll indicated." (*New York Times,* May 27, 2021).

---

17   "Why is America So Divided Today?" *Time,* January 16, 2021
*   "How did you go bankrupt? Two ways. Gradually, then suddenly." Earnest Hemingway.

Some of the old Us. vs. Them fractures persist as well: tribalism; the pretentious arrogance and intolerance of the left and the sheer - nowadays especially - Neanderthal ignorance of the right and the divisive, inflammatory rhetoric of both.

Most distressing is the "my way or the highway" orthodoxy of both left and right. It is utterly antithetical to what forged the Constitution and birthed a nation. Compromise leads to consensus and to governing.

Yet what remains so positively striking about the United States is that no people on earth - of whatever persuasion - struggle more mightily and openly with contentious issues than do Americans. Some struggles, culminated in a Civil War. Others - civil rights, the war in Vietnam - were fought in the streets. Still others were waged in courts of law.
What is so worrisome now, is that the "fractious and mean-spiritedness" is unprecedented in our history.
Viewed from the perspective of our history, Us. vs. Them clashes between Americans during turbulent times isn't a new phenomenon. Every decade is replete with noisy encounters of opposing points of view. But this time. it has gone beyond noisy encounters.

Why?
> "Hell is empty and all the devils are here."[18]

You know who they are: look no further than these pages. They are in plain sight. The most insidious of the devils are the GOP coat and tie, pantsuit-wearing, bottom feeders in Congress.

I hope and pray, that we haven't lost our common bond and citizenship with each other. If we have, then Samuel Johnson's words give me an immense foreboding for our beloved country.

---

[18]   William Shakespeare, *The Tempest*

The Georgia Follies

Satire, being levelled at all, is never resented for offence by any.

Jonathan Swift

"In high school, I discovered that I had the gift of laughter and of making others laugh too. I also developed the elusive art of conversation and learned that I could easily engage all manner of people. I was never the shy type. I came to like being the center of attention and with it, came my need for the Four A's: Acceptance. Affirmation. Approval. Applause. Humor always played a part of that need."[19]

That humor made its stage debut when I started performing stand-up comedy. I wrote my own monologues and found I had a flair for writing comedy too. I was especially drawn to writing satirical pieces. "The Georgia Follies" was born and appeared in 2009 in my first book.1

Here are five selections from that first edition; it might elicit a smile or chuckle or two:

> With Governor Sonny Perdue term-limited from seeking re-election next year, there's already talk about what he plans to do. Sources close to the governor say there's a wide range of options including joining the circus as a clown, teaching trout fishing to inner-city youth, or being a spokesman for the Women's Christian Temperance Union.

> A headline that would piss-off Amnesty International: "Troy Davis Executed." Death penalty opponents blame racism and Bush.

> Another cheerful headline: "Bravo cancels Real Housewives of Atlanta." The housewives have been booked for a limited engagement at Zoo Atlanta.

> Tommy Irvin, the longest-serving Commissioner of Agriculture in the United States as well as the longest-serving statewide official in Georgia is said to be close to deciding whether or not he'll seek re-election next year. Observers say Irwin will make an announcement as soon as he hears from

---

[19]   Charles Jackson, "Stand Up," *I Didn't Ask To Be Here*, 2019

General Lee on the specific terms of the surrender signed at Appomattox Courthouse.

> Former Georgia congressman and House Speaker Newt Gingrich has again denied reports that he's running for president in 2012. However, he did indicate that a Coronation would work nicely.

Now, we fast forward to 2021…

The Georgia Follies, 2021 Edition

> Major League Baseball is being sued over its move of July's All-Star game out of Atlanta.
On June 1, a 21-page lawsuit by a conservative small-business advocacy organization was filed in federal court in New York. The suit demands the immediate return of the game to Atlanta and $100 million in damages to local and state small businesses. The suit also seeks $1 billion in punitive damages to be distributed equally to Republican members of the Georgia legislature.

> Mayor Keisha Lance Bottoms' exit from the Atlanta mayor's race makes the November contest wide open. City Hall observers said the growing number of candidates – notable for consisting of has-beens and perennial losers – is likely to force a run-off between Bad and Worst.

> Former Senator Kelly Loeffler is looking for a multi-year deal to be a store window mannequin.

> Former Senator David Perdue is reportedly working as a stunt dummy for Tyler Perry Studios.

> A cheerful headline: "Bravo Cancels Real Housewives of Atlanta." The housewives have been booked for a limited engagement at Zoo Atlanta.

> Emory University has closed again today because of continued massive student strikes led by Madonna. Among other demands, the students - many with New Jersey license plates - are calling for the construction of a new chapel dedicated to "The Vagina Monologues" and extension of the afternoon cocktail hour with seven-days-a-week maid service.

> Voting rights activist Stacey Abrams and Governor Brian Kemp were married in a simple ceremony at Sweet Auburn BBQ. The bride wore a white tux pantsuit; the groom traditional African wedding attire.

> A couple in Savannah, who met during the pandemic, were seen tenderly removing each other's mask straps for the first time.

> Congresswoman Marjorie Taylor Greene's new book, *Dangers to America: Gay Southern Baptists, Jewish Space Aliens,* was released to mixed reviews.

Greene's next book, *My Life As A Trans Nazi* is due out in September.

> A doctor in Athens, was required to inform a woman – and rabid Dawgs fan- seeking an abortion that the fetus was already a Tech Yellow Jackets fan.

> And news from another campus: Georgia State University, has added several other offenses - in addition to incidents of racism, sexism and homophobia - students can report to the hotline number (404) 666-TELL. The new hotline offenses are inappropriate laughter, actually reading a book, use of the words "conservative," "Anglo-Saxon" or uttering the name Winston Churchill.

> And this just in: Sonny Perdue has his sights set on becoming Chancellor of the University System of Georgia. He defends his quest as necessary for him to stay relevant. He was recently featured in the widely touted YouTube video, with cousin David Perdue and Kelly Loeffler, in *Dumb, Dumber and Dumbest.*

> The Georgia Republican Party held its annual convention in a tightly packed dumpster outside a landfill in Crawfordville, the county seat of Taliaferro County, population 1,611 (est. 2019). The convention unanimously passed several resolutions including reaffirmation that God is an elderly, white gentleman with a long beard; Critical Race Theory is a Marxist plot and that absentee voting in Georgia must include drug testing, as well as blood, urine and stool samples.

"You can't make up anything anymore. The world itself is a satire. All you're doing is recording it."
Art Buchwald

That's all folks!

Now What?

He who has a 'why' to live, can bear with almost any 'how'.

Friedrich Nietzsche

Now What? Or making sense of being here, although I didn't ask to be.

For starters, some sage advice from Stanley Kubrick:

"The most terrifying fact about the universe is not that it is hostile but that it is indifferent, but if we can come to terms with this indifference, then our existence as a species can have genuine meaning. However vast the darkness, *we must supply our own light.*" Indeed.

"As I amble as serenely as possible through my later years, I come back to the absolutely stunning realization of my life being *illuminated by the steady radiance, renewed daily, of a wonder the source of which is beyond all reason.*"[20]

That ambling "serenely as possible" has been a chore at times. I have three distinct and conflicting emotions: *second childhood, serenity and sheer terror.*

"Throughout Western history scholars and writers have characterized old age as a period of a second childhood and childish behavior: Sophocles, 'A man growing old becomes a child again.' The second childhood was also interpreted as a stage of life where the life cycle returned to its beginning."[21]

My second childhood - child-like abandon - is a daily romp free from earlier cares and wants. *Simple pleasures delight me* and a sense of calm and freedom envelopes my being. Goethe, as usual, says it best:

"Age is no second childhood - age makes plain,

Children we were, true children we remain." (*Faust*).

---

[20]   Charles Jackson, "Oh Wow!" *I Didn't Ask To Be Here,* 2019

[21]   "A Return to Infancy: Old Age and the Second Childhood in History" *SAGE Journal,* March 1, 1993

I find that aging brings with it a certain serenity. There is grace and stateliness with age. What really matters as we age is not the condition of the body, but that of the spirit. And yet…

My terror is best expressed by this line, "There is no impurity more impure than old age."[22] The medical issues attendant with aging are real and so is the stark realization that time waits for no man. Bette Davis put it more bluntly, "Old age ain't no place for sissies!"

A great friend passed on an email about aging and it concludes with this:

"So, take some rest, chill, stay cool, eat, drink and enjoy your life." I'll drink to that.

"I know I have a sense of personal well being.
I know I play the hand I was dealt.
I know I am the best possible Charles Jackson I can be.
I know the past is over and the future is not yet.
I know the here and now matters most.
I know I have demons but my angels prevail in the end.
I know I am in this world but not bound to it because I know I am on higher ground."

In the introduction to *I Didn't Ask To Be Here,* I enumerated those eight elements of my being. Two
years later, they remain at the core of my reality: wedded to spirituality and a rediscovered Christian faith.

Kierkegaard said, *"Life is not a problem to be solved, but a reality to be experienced."* I am experiencing my self-actualized reality.

I claim no divine insight, no self-help mantra or guru-like psycho babble. That said, based solely on my own living reality, the essence of Now What is having:

A sense of self.
A sense of place.
A sense of transcendence.

---

[22]   Thomas Mann, *Death in Venice,* 1912

Every person must find his or her own Now What? It is a journey, not a destination. It is imperative to realize one's own living reality, with the mantra: *I am a human being, My life matters.* Without that, all is lost.

As we make that journey of discovery, it is prudent to be mindful of:

"As our planet rotates around the sun, we are all space riders on that same planet Earth. Enjoy the ride. In the twinkling of an eye, it will end…for each and every rider and eventually the Earth itself. My (our) ticket to ride has an expiration date. Death and life are inseparable; they support each other.

At the moment, when that ticket is punched and my ride has expired here, I shall return from whence I came, exclaiming:

'My God, it's full of stars!'
Oh wow![23]

I am.

Charles Jackson, Atlanta, Georgia, June 2021

*****

---

[23] Charles Jackson, "Oh Wow!" *I Didn't Ask To Be Here,* 2019
In Arthur C. Clarke's magnificent book, *2001: A Space Odyssey* (1968), Dr. Dave Bowman's famous line and final words as he entered the monolith were, "My God, it's full of stars!"

Acknowledgments

The author would like to thank two accomplished and esteemed friends for their support and encouragement again in helping to make another book possible: James A. Taylor, of considerable literary reputation, with his wise counsel and the brilliant Eric Wardowski, for his help with all things computer-related including formatting the book.

Charles Jackson, is a native-born, white Southerner, possessing male genitalia. Despite those obstacles, he has soldiered on. His greatest life achievements were in elementary school when he was awarded the prestigious Fifth Grade *Penmanship Award* and in high school, as the author and sole proprietor of his eleventh-grade book, *Gems of Inspiration*, said to rank with the greatest unpublished works in Western Civilization. Mr. Jackson is a history buff, political junkie, avid reader and sports fan. A self-described unrepentant Anglophile and born again Episcopalian, he is working at retired and lives in the Promised Land, his beloved South, in Atlanta, Georgia.

APPENDIX OF QUOTATIONS

Overleaf
Heaven's light forever shines. Earth shadows fly. Life, like a dome of many colored glass, stains the white Radiance of Eternity, until Death tramples it to fragments. Die if thou wouldst be with That which Thou dost seek.
Percy Bysshe Shelley

The two most important days in your life are the day you are born and the day you find out why.
Mark Twain

Introduction   **1**
The universe appears every moment through the portal, 'I am.'
Ramana Maharshi

Virus   **5**
Death has come up into our windows, it has entered our palaces, to cut off the children from the streets and the young men from the squares.
Jeremiah 9:20

Divide   **9**
Rich fellas come up an' they die, an' their kids ain't no good an' they die out. But we keep a'comin'. We're the people that live. They can't wipe us out; they can't lick us. We'll go on forever, Pa, 'cause we're the people.
John Steinbeck, *The Grapes of Wrath* (Ma Joad)

Donald Trump   **13**
His mother should have thrown him away and kept the stork.
Mae West

Know Nothing   **15**
If we were a dog food, they would take us off the shelf.
Former Congressman Tom Davis (R-Virginia)

Newspeak   **19**
Of all tyrannies, a tyranny sincerely exercised for the good of its victims may be the most oppressive. It would be better to live under robber barons than under omnipotent moral busybodies. The robber baron's cruelty may sometimes sleep, his cupidity may at some point be satiated; but those who

torment us for our own good will torment us without end for they do so with the approval of their own conscience. They may be more likely to go to Heaven yet at the same time likelier to make a Hell of earth. This very kindness stings with intolerable insult. To be "cured" against one's will and cured of states which we may not regard as disease is to be put on a level of those who have not yet reached the age of reason or those who never will; to be classed with infants, imbeciles, and domestic animals.

C.S. Lewis

You Betcha Doggone It!   23
You Betcha Doggone It!

Sarah Palin

Fear   27
The only thing we have to fear is...fear itself — nameless, unreasoning, unjustified terror ...

Franklin D. Roosevelt

Us vs. Them   31
When once the forms of civility are violated, there remains little hope of return to kindness or decency.

Samuel Johnson

The Georgia Follies   35
Satire, being levelled at all, is never resented for offence by any.

Jonathan Swift

Now What?   39
He who has a 'why' to live, can bear with almost any 'how'.

Friedrich Nietzsche

*****

www.ingramcontent.com/pod-product-compliance
Lightning Source LLC
Chambersburg PA
CBHW061528250726
48657CB00005B/2133